Do
Computer Byte?

Written by Martin Hopper
Illustrated by Ken Hardy

Published by
Walrus Productions
Seattle

Published by Walrus Productions
4805 NE 106th St. Seattle, WA 98125
(206) 364-4365
e-mail walrus@aa.net
www.aa.net/walrus

Written by Martin Hopper
Illustrated by Ken Hardy
Layout and typography The Durland Group

Printed by Vaughan Printing, Nashville, Tennessee

Library of Congress Catalog Card Number 98-60802

Hopper, Martin
Does Your Computer Byte? / by Martin Hopper ; Illustrated by Ken Hardy

ISBN 0-9635176-6-X
1. Computers-Humor. 2.Internet--Humor, Pictorial. I. Title

Printed in the United States of America

10 9 8 7 6 5 4 3 2 1

Dedicated to
all computer users...

because sooner or later
your computer will byte

The Bits & Pieces Inside

Error
Please press
OK or CANCEL
to continue...
Yes
No

☺ Love at First Byte ☹

The computer bug has bitten - but was it love at first byte? Or is it a love/hate relationship? We love the worlds opened by our computers, but those "fatal system errors" can be a kiss of death to any relationship. So sit back and read on while you wait for your system to pickup the pieces and get back to where you were a few hours ago.

Why is that "out-of-the-box" experience always a surprise?

WITH
CARE
MONITOR

Just think!

It wasn't long ago
we wanted to keep mice
"off" our desk tops

Warning:

No matter how
many times you hit "escape"
... you'll still be **here**

ESC

Computer Literacy

In today's world it seems everyone from employers, to dates, to your mother-in-law wants to know if you are computer literate.

We think we are - but are you sure?

"An optimist says the hard drive is half full
A pessimist says it's half empty
The computer literate will upgrade anyway"

You probably aren't computer literate if you think a ***hot boot*** is what you get when you sit too close to a fire

You probably aren't
computer literate if you hear
SCSI (Skuzzy)
and think about people
who hang out at the bus depot

SCSI
TO BUSES
SO, WHERE YA HEADIN'?

You probably aren't
computer literate if you think
installing a ***patch***
is how you fix a flat tire

You probably aren't
computer literate if you think
server is
politically correct for waitress

BILL G'S
N. T.
DINER
JOE
FLO

You most definitely aren't
computer literate if you think
CD's relate only to banking
and that **ATM**
only means a cash machine

or if you think that
hot-links
are only for breakfast
or that
RISC is just a board game

If you think a **Webmaster** is something to do with spiders... you're still not computer literate.

You probably aren't computer literate if you think **cache** is spent at the computer store to buy more memory

A **cache overflow** is definitely not like a visit from Ed McMahan

You probably aren't
computer literate if you think
a **raster image**
relates to reggae musicians

You probably aren't computer literate if you think **Spam**® only comes in a can

Spam is a registered trademark of the Hormel Foods Corp

SPUT!
SPAM

What is the icon for ⌘ Obsolete ⌘

It always seems that no matter how much you spend, or how hot the technology is, as soon as you set up that new computer, it's obsolete, one step from shelfware. Why does everything that's "New" suddenly seem like a rusted-out smoke-belching old Dodge that is just taking up space on the information superhighway.

Now I know
why it runs
so slow
NEW

Can't afford
faster computers?

Hire slower workers!

*That way the computers
will at least seem faster*

You know it's time
to replace your system
if the <u>clock speed</u> is
<u>less</u> than its "*age in days*"

Grandpa, please tell us again about the days when computer users were considered counter-culture icons

You really should upgrade
if you are using "save"
as an oven timer

It's embarrassing
when you can't even find
a charity that will take your old
computer as a donation

NEW COMPUTER
GREAT, THAT'S THREE

You know it's time to replace
your computer system
if you hit 3 stop lights
bringing it home from the store!

You really know it's time
to replace your computer
if you still remember "Basic"
... *and have to use it*

Actually ... you know it's time
to replace your computer
when Bill Gates
thinks you should

Remember when...

"Log On" was
adding more wood to the fire

"Windows" were made of glass

"Cursers" used profanity

"Keyboards" were pianos

"Hard Drives"
were long trips in a car

"Applications" were what you filled out when you needed a job

"Programs" were TV shows

"Backups" only happened in your toilet

You Always Need
$ More Stuff $

Owning a computer can lead to compulsions. They're not always curable and treatments are often expensive.

The symptoms may include: eye bulging, salivation, the repetition of phrases such as; I gotta getta scanner. I gotta getta a modem. I gotta getta internet provider. I gotta getta more memory. I gotta getta a new computer.

FRAGILE
HANDLE WITH CARE

Moore's Law (restated)

Hardware requirements
double faster than your budget

Gate's Corollary

My software will *always* be bigger than your hardware

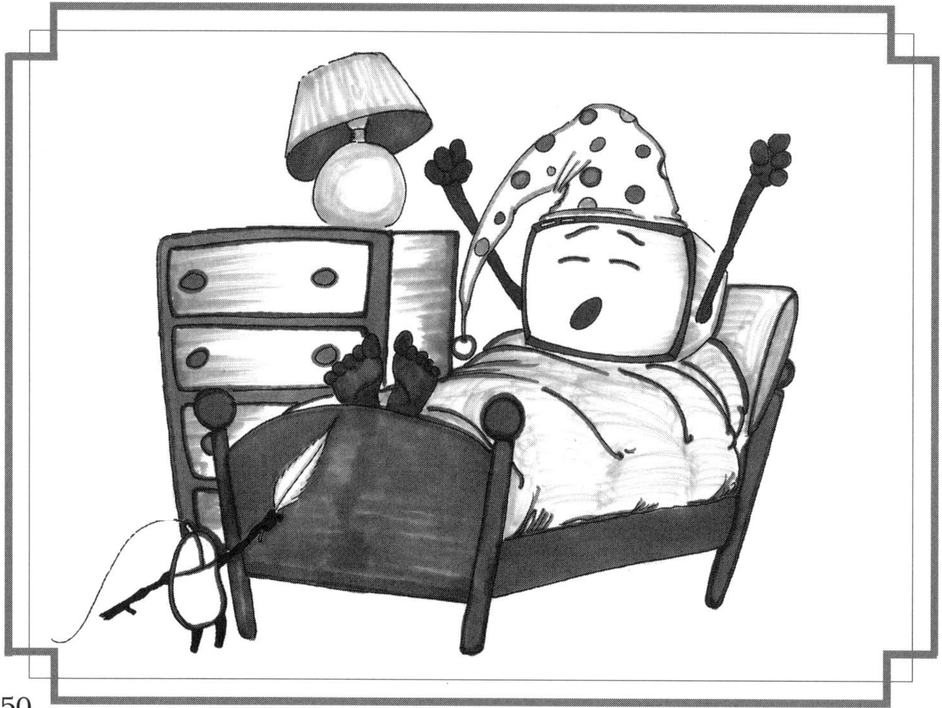

No matter what they tell you,
embedded applications
don't need comforters

Remember
the secret to happiness is:

Always get more **RAM**
than you can afford,
...no matter what it takes!

WILL
WORK FOR
RAM

"Mine is bigger
than yours"

It's not the size
of your computer...
but how you use it!

Macs vs PC's

An age old battle - full of villains and heroes each side wearing the banner of righteousness, but who will win? Some say the battle is long over, others say it's just begun - all that is known for sure is that both camps are still punching and the round is not over.

Was the apple in the Garden of Eden a Macintosh?

The day when
Microsoft and Apple
merge to become "Applesoft"

...Pigs really will fly

Windows '98
proves that Elvis lives!

If Windows '95 = Apple '89
is Java
still just a cup of Joe?

Stockholders of Apple Computer probably think that "windows" would have been better off with curtains

User Friendly?

Each time the computer world finds a way to make things even more user friendly it seems life gets more and more complex. Somebody once said, "Build a fool-proof system and only a fool would want to use it."

Now to make life easy, wouldn't it be wonderful if there was a special dialog button that really could make all your troubles go away?

I think we are there!

solutions
Your computer will now permanently shut down and not restart
OK

Some day will software
become so powerful
that it actually could blow up?

You have to wonder ...

Wouldn't it sometimes
"feel great"
to *really boot* your computer?

KAPOW!
BEEP
BLAM
YAAAGH!
TAK
TAK
TAK
TAK
TAK

Computers:

Why are they called "personal" when you always have to wait in line to use them?

The old expression
"to err is human"

...really describes
a computer problem

Your Error Table

90	error	DestDefect, Destination disc needs a passport
91	error	ISPDisCon, ISP doesn't really care
92	error	ISPBusy, You chose the wrong ISP
93	error	InsufRam, min configuration is never enough
94	error	TooMuchRam, nothing to do with memory
95	error	JavaSoft, I didn't want decaf
96	error	Javahard, Too much espresso: CPU is fuzzy
97	error	TooManyDisks, Should have got a zip drive
98	error	DiskFull, Did you think 10GB was enough?
99	error	DiskError, You should have done a backup
9A	error	LogicBad, Your CPU inhaled
9B	error	LogicOverflow, Too many FAQ's: no answers
9C	error	LogicUnderflow, You should have upgraded

Yikes !

Some computer problems require "alternative medicine"

♋ Virtual Fantasy ♋

Why do we go
to so much trouble
to create virtual reality
when a child only has to dream?

Virtual Reality:

No matter how good it becomes,
there are some things
that are much better in real life

Computers and the Church

Can computers produce a virtual reality that will replace the church? Although some say visiting a web site may be more efficient than actually attending church, we don't agree.

Here are a couple of questions you must ask:

1. At a virtual Mass is the net a fisher of souls?
2. Is the Eucharist the ultimate virtual reality?
3. Is the computer really an instrument of Satan?
4. Does God really have a web site? How about e-mail?

Is life ... a beta for Heaven?

Betas are versions of software
that are released to selected members
of the public for testing
before the final version is sold.

If you fail the beta of life,
the final version
may never be issued

Virtual games gone too far

Is virtual reality
mind-candy for the masses?

Why worry about
global warming, taxes, nuclear
war and overpopulation
when you can go online?

The Internet

The Internet is like the world's largest community, except no one is in charge. You can just walk in and build a home (site) or open a business any time of day or night. The only road maps are your trusty browser and a little luck. The first time you use the Internet you'll wonder why you bothered. But the more you use it, the better it gets - until someone points out that you've been on-line all day and still haven't found what you were looking for.

Forget all the hype...
the next big breakthrough
will be how to make the
World Wide Web relevant
to the rest of the world

Be Prepared:

When wandering the wilds
of the World Wide Web,
don't be surprised if that
mountain of information
you were hoping to find
is somewhere else

WWW.KNOWLEDGE.COM
THIS SITE HAS MOVED
!, ?

Give a man a fish
and you feed him for a day

Teach him to use the "Net" and
he won't bother you for weeks

One of the great
satisfactions of e-mail
is being able to empty the trash
and not add to a land fill

Net Neophytes:

You can always count on them to *immediately* call and ask, "Did you get my e-mail?"

You
Got
Mail

ZZZZZZZZZ
WWW TV
CH 1002
4:37
CHEEZE
SCULPTURES

WWW TV:

57,000,000 channels and nothin's on

On big days, you can always expect that surfin' the Net will be a little crowded

It's all too easy
while surfing the Net
to arrive at the opposite place
than you needed to go to

WRONG LOCATION
SITE MOVED

Surfing the Net lets you visit
all kinds of people
you'd rather not meet in person

Is the Net merely a way for the
socially retarded to avoid going
face to face with the world?

With all the scams
on the Web, many URL's
ought to end with **.con**

When people
abuse the Internet:

They should be placed
under "**mouse arrest**"

BUGS BUGS BUGS

The term "bugs" dates back to the first days of computing (with vacuum tubes) when an airborne invasion could bring the whole system down. Even though we've never seen a screen door on a PC, the term has stuck. Of course when a bug strikes, your friendly tech support folks have never quite heard of one like yours before - it must have originated in their competitor's product - the one they say you should never have installed...

?sgub naem ayaddahW

!sgub yna evah t'nseod metsys sihT

A computer will crash whenever you make a fatal error ...be careful

Remember, you can always blame it on your software

F8LERROR

POISO
EXTERM

Here's my bug problem
can you really help?

There is only one sure way
to eliminate all the bugs
from your computer

You'll never get
a speeding ticket on the
information superhighway
with an analog phone line

Contrarians

Although some of us have to have the latest and greatest, there are many others who take great pleasure in heading in the opposite direction. They love to point out how smoothly their ancient system operates, how simple legacy languages were and how the last time they saw a bug was out in the garden. Someone really needs to tell these people that computers aren't just for work ... PLEASE!

Computer Consultant:

Knows exactly what
any piece of software can do,
but has never actually used it

The shortest unit of time
is...

The Ohnosecond

The length of time it takes to realize
you just made a big mistake!

NEVER NEVER NEVER...

let your computer know
you're in a hurry

Are dumb terminals stupid?

And are the promoters of "network computers" smart enough to remember dumb terminals?

Been There, Done That!

When you see the latest integrated multi-media system, remember that it's all been done before.

The first integrated multi-media system was the Coleco Adam: introduced in 1983, it used a cassette player for storage and sold for about $200. In 1985 the multi-media Commodore Amiga 1000 featured a windowing operating system.

Never Mind...

"I think there is a world market for maybe five computers"
Thomas Watson, chairman of IBM, 1943

"Computers in the future may weigh no more than 1.5 tons"
Popular Mechanics, forecasting the future of science, 1949

"I have talked with the best people, and I can assure you that data processing is a fad that won't last out the year"
The editor in charge of business books for Prentice Hall, 1957

"But what is it good for?"
Engineer at the Advanced Computing Systems Division of IBM, commenting on the microchip, 1968.

"There's no reason anyone would want a computer in their home"
Ken Olson, founder of Digital Equipment, 1977

Never get in a flame war
with a touch typist

Flame wars are easier to start
than to end - even with :-)s

Is a flame war with an idiot
an endless do-loop?

"I accidently faxed you the entire Internet"

Remember...
The power only goes off when you haven't "backed up" your work!

But don't worry...
your backup probably won't work anyway

Who's the Boss?

In many ways the computer has taken control of our lives, Although we think computers were fully under our control when we first made them, things may have got out of hand...

But at least they can't delete US yet.

SVEEE

Does Microsoft
have a MIS department
and does it want to centralize
control of all *their* PC's?

Before you embrace the NC
or the Net PC, please
remember it may be a plot
by the MIS department to take
control of you again

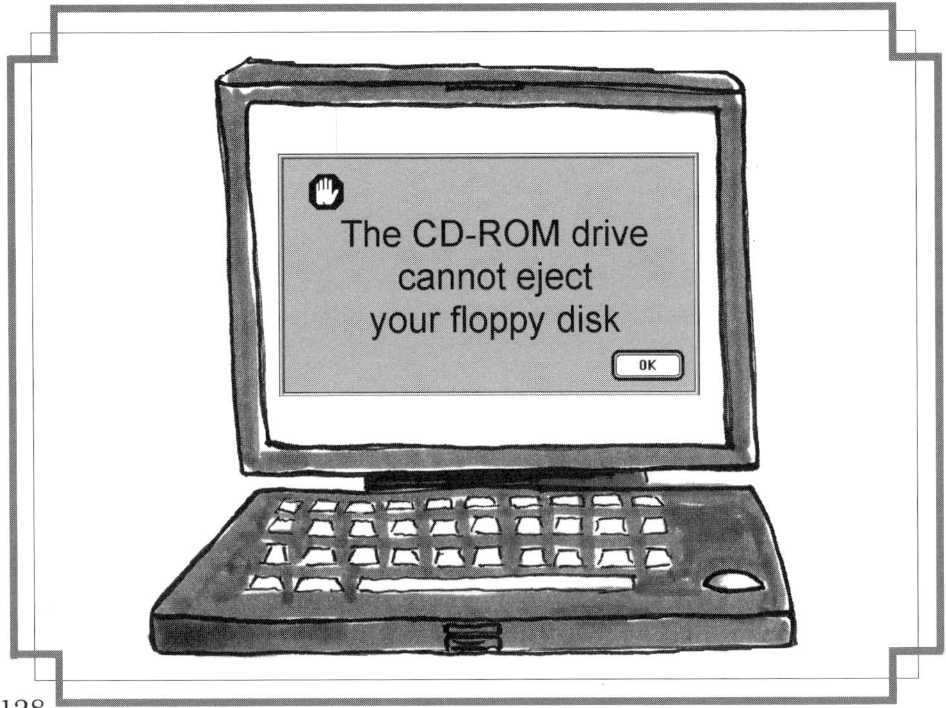
The CD-ROM drive
cannot eject
your floppy disk
OK

Computers are literalists:

They do what you say,
not what you meant!

RAM DISK
is not an installation procedure

You'll never amount to much
if you always say "Yes" to
...Play Another Game?

Wow ... Far Out Man

If the computer was the key
to the paperless office,
why do we now
buy paper by the case?

If computers
are laborsaving devices,
why do they take so much work?

This year when you pay taxes:

Will your computer be
a business expense
or a dependent?

Office Networks

Everywhere we turn, the office, school and even at home, people are connecting their home computers into networks. LANs, WANs and even out to the Internet. Just imagine a dozen computers flashing "General Protection Fault" all at once! ... and it's all in the name of productivity.

If NC means
Not Compatible
and
Net PC means
Net Perpetually Crashing

Does NT mean
Never Trusted?

Remember:
Networks take thin clients
and fat servers

If you think
your network is safe because
you've got firewall routers,
remember ... the Fire Marshall
rates firewalls by hours,
not years

When you load information on your network, remember your communication is merely value-added electricity

The "Help Desk" explained:

Press 1 if you want 3
Press 4 if you want 2
Press 6 if you want 5

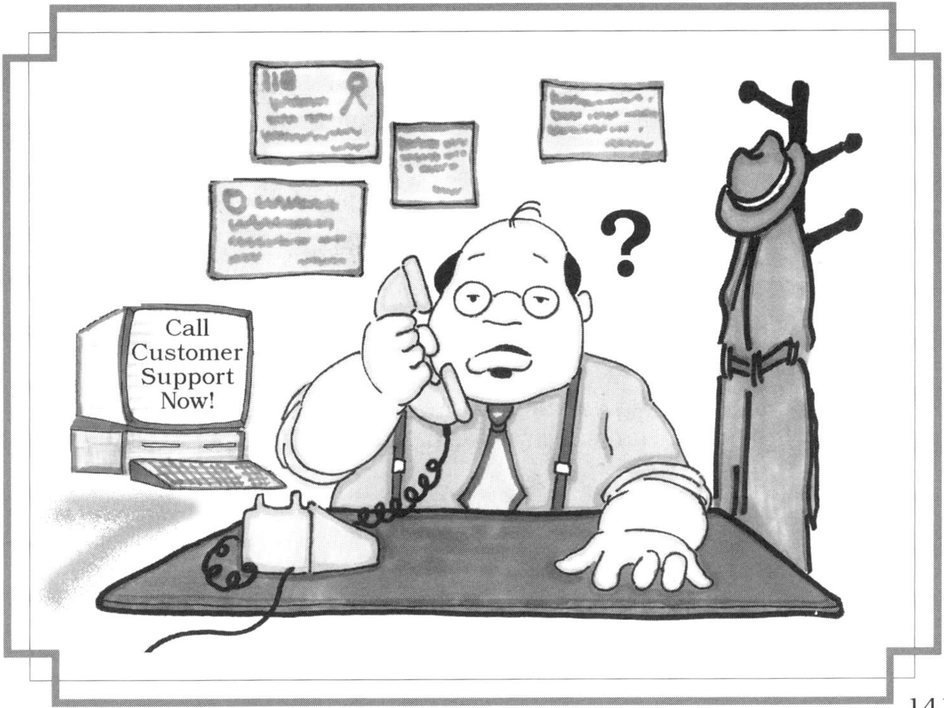
Call
Customer
Support
Now!

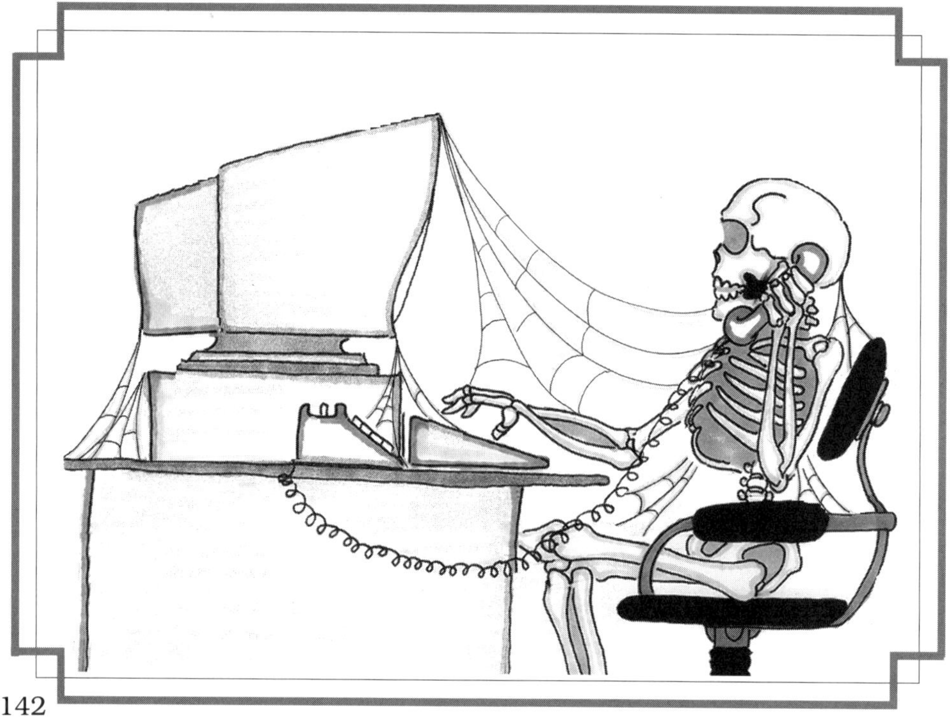

"Please continue to hold,
your call is very important to us,
a tech support representative
will be right with you"

The Future and Beyond

If you were to consult with an oracle to see the future of computing, the answer you seek will depend, as usual, on the marketing department's latest whim and never ever on common sense... Just ask Dilbert!

Trends seem to go in cycles and last year's dumb idea may just as well become next year's stroke of genius.

WINDOWS
2020
INSTALL
DIRECTLY TO
BRAIN

If engineers ran the marketing department you'd have no more "vaporware" ...but your company would likely be out of business!

And if you think "vaporware"
is a recent phenomenon...
read the Book of Revelations

Format C:/U
does not equal
order out of chaos.

Even in real life
CTRL+ALT+DEL
won't always
give you a fresh start

BIG
I.S.P.

Telecommuting is great...
except for traffic jams on the
information superhighway.

WWW
really can mean the
"World Wide Wait"

Breakthrough technology:

Real protection against unauthorized access

You'll know the Web has finally become a real moneymaker when they perfect 1-900 URL's

If you haven't "upgraded"
because you're waiting for
technology to stabilize,
...you never will

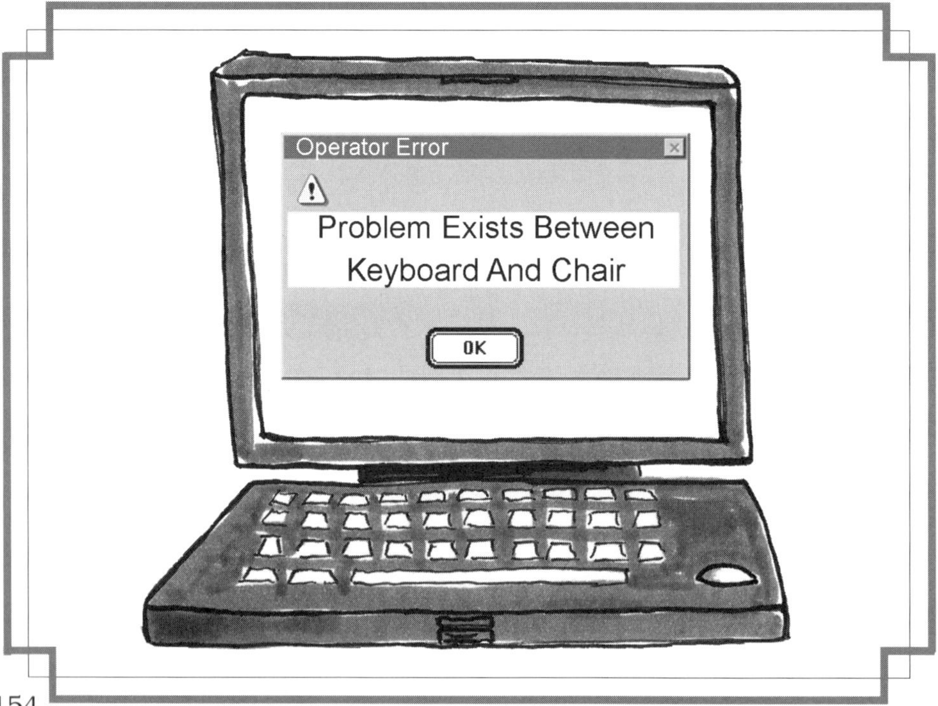
Operator Error
Problem Exists Between Keyboard And Chair
OK

The End

Glossary

ATM	Asynchronous Transfer Mode - still need cache to move data
Cache	Memory reserved to hold data for subsequent processing - your computers waiting room
CPU	Central Processing Unit - your PC's brains
FAQs	Frequently Asked Questions - Like Joe Friday said, "Just the FAQs, ma'am"
FORTRAN	A legacy (old) language favored by engineers
Hot Boot	Restarting your computer without turning the power off
Hot Links	Takes you to another Web Page by clicking text
ISP	Internet Service Provider - Your Internet connection when it's not busy
MIS	Management Information Systems Department - still jealous of PC's after two decades

Patch	A program written to make another program work - Duct tape for software
RAM	Random Access Memory - the working memory of your PC - always in short supply
RASTER	Bitmap images - small squares that represent graphics
RISC	Reduced Instruction Set Computing - you still need more RAM!
SCSI	Small Computer System Interface - the connection between computer, printer and scanner etc.
Server	Stores data & controls communications for networks
Shelfware	Obsolete computer hardware or software that is set aside and no longer used.
Spam	Bulk unsolicited e-mail, annoying, never satisfying
URL	Universal Reference Locator - real Web addresses, even when not found
Webmaster	WebSite designer, HTML guru, HTML junkie, God

ABOUT THE AUTHOR

Martin Hopper resides in San Jose, California, the capital of Silicon Valley, with his wife & two children. He believes that the best way to improve the performance of your computer is to approach it with an open mind and a keen sense of humor.

ABOUT THE ILLUSTRATOR

Ken Hardy lives in Seattle, Washington. The spark of his passion for art began at age two. He now works as a freelance illustrator - including computer game animation.

OTHER FUN BOOKS

A whimsical collection of delightful books to make you think, chuckle, self-motivate & lift your spirits.

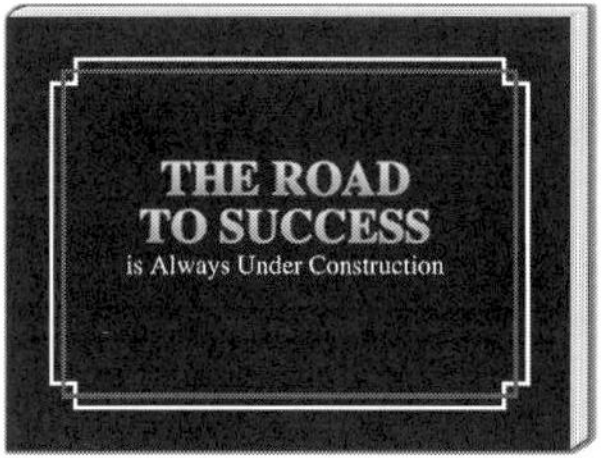

Road to Success

Motherhood

Doggie Tales

Money

View from Litter Box

Kitty Litterature